Swim, Fish, Swim!

by Vica Tantsioura

I0436289

To all children, with lots of love

Text and illustrations copyright © 2012 by Vica Tantsioura.
All rights reserved.

Little **Fish**

lives in a **big** ocean,

Where creatures stay in constant motion,
Smaller fish are swimming away

From bigger ones,
who are after their prey.

Hungry Fish
wants to devour

Zooplankton every hour.
Fry and krill are food to him.
To get more food, Fish has to swim!

Hungry lobster wants to eat
Every little Fish he'll meet.

Poor Fish! What can help him?
Swim, Fish, swim! Swim, Fish, swim!

Eagle ray soars out to crack

Little lobster he'll attack.

Lucky Fish! The ray helped him!
Go on, Fish! Swim, Fish, swim!

Hungry squid would like to seize
Every little Fish he sees.

Poor Fish! What can help him?
Swim, Fish, swim! Swim, Fish, swim!

Moray eel darts out to seize
Every little Fish he sees.

Poor Fish! What can help him?
Swim, Fish, swim! Swim, Fish, swim!

Five-lined snapper wants to seize
Every little Fish he sees.
Poor Fish! What can help him?

Swim, Fish, swim!
Swim, Fish, swim!

Hungry bull shark wants to seize
Every little Fish he sees.

Poor Fish! What can help him?
Swim, Fish, swim! Swim, Fish, swim!

Hungry tuna wants to seize
Every little Fish he sees.

Poor Fish! What can help him?
Swim, Fish, swim! Swim, Fish, swim!

Hungry bull shark quickly eats
Any tuna fish he meets.

Lucky Fish! The shark helped him.
Keep up, Fish! Swim, Fish, swim!

Hungry dolphin wants to seize
Every little Fish he sees.

Poor Fish! What can help him?
Swim, Fish, swim! Swim, Fish, swim!

Hungry white gull wants to seize
Every little Fish he sees.
Poor Fish! What can help him?
Swim, Fish, swim! Swim, Fish, swim!

The sun goes down.

The night falls over the big ocean.
The fish can't stay in rapid motion,
The fish can't see what's floating by…
How does the fish stay alive?

Hide, Fish, hide!

To hide himself away,
Fish finds a tiny cave,
He closes his eyes tight-tight
And sleeps in peace all night.

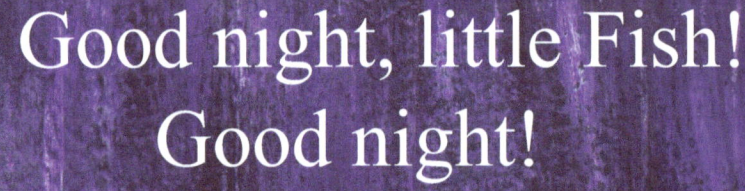

Good night, little Fish!
Good night!

www.ingramcontent.com/pod-product-compliance
Lightning Source LLC
Chambersburg PA
CBHW060805290526
45792CB00005BA/1537

9781480234406